Old ALLOA

by
Guthrie Hutton

Bandmaster A. Smith with the Alloa Salvation Army band in 1925.

THE PUBLISHERS REGRET THAT THEY CANNOT SUPPLY
COPIES OF ANY PICTURES FEATURED IN THIS BOOK.

ACKNOWLEDGEMENTS
I would like to thank Bob McCutcheon, Peter Stewart and Stuart Marshall for providing so
many of the pictures for this book. It is no exaggeration to say that I could not have done it
without them. Thanks also to Hugh Brodie for providing the picture on page 26.

Park School, designed by William Kerr in 1935, is in the foreground of this view looking across Alloa to the Ochil Hills.

INTRODUCTION

Alloa's growth as an industrial centre had much more to do with people than with place. Located on a tidally difficult river estuary, with only the mouth of a small burn as a harbour, it had no obvious advantages for shipping. Its castle even lacked the natural defences enjoyed by the neighbouring stronghold at Clackmannan, but it was the family who inhabited the castle, the Erskines of Mar, who made the difference.

Sir Robert Erskine was granted the lands of Alloa and surrounding area in 1368 for service to King David II, and succeeding generations of the family continued to serve Scottish royalty, forming close ties with the Stewart dynasty. That relationship could have halted Alloa's industrial development in its tracks when the 6th Earl of Mar led the Jacobite cause in 1715 and had to flee the country after suffering defeat at the Battle of Sheriffmuir. 'Bobbing John', as he was nicknamed, was a remarkable man. He created the Gartmorn Dam to provide power to expand his coal mines, developed the harbour and had a Customs House established.

Who knows what else he would have achieved had religion and politics not tragically have robbed Alloa, and Scotland, of his energy and vision. Fortunately the setback proved only temporary. The 6th Earl's brother bought the forfeited estates and restored them to the family, allowing future generations to start a glassworks in 1750 and lay one of Scotland's earliest railways, a wagonway, from the mines near Sauchie to the harbour about 1766. Alloa's progress restarted just at the time that the population of Scotland's central lowlands was growing and creating a demand for the products of industry. With its excellent coal supplies and improved harbour, Alloa was well placed to meet the demand and new industries, notably those producing beer and processing wool, were attracted to the town.

There were other factors too. Good water supplies and the availability of barley from the carselands and Fife encouraged George Younger to set up his Meadow Brewery in the 1760s. Others followed and Alloa grew to become a brewing centre matched in Scotland only by Edinburgh. Wool was also available locally and about 1813 John Paton set up a yarn-spinning business in a building in the old town. He went on to establish Kilncraigs Mill which grew to become a huge concern, spinning knitting wool and yarns. The firm merged with J. & J. Baldwin of Halifax in 1924 to become Patons & Baldwins Ltd.

Such was the scale of Alloa's industrial progress that it swept past Clackmannan as the wee county's big town to become its administrative centre. It remains the county town in all but name, but despite that hit hard times in the late twentieth century as one by one the great industries fell victim to the harsh economic climate of the time. Alloa has been left to search for new beginnings, but it has done that before and who would bet against it succeeding again.

The Auld Brig

3

Old buildings crowded in on the old road to the town green that ran across the bridge over the Brothie Burn seen on the previous page. Through the nineteenth and early twentieth centuries this old town became isolated as the commercial town centre developed to the north and industry grew to the south. Sandwiched between such inexorable pressures, many characterful vernacular buildings disappeared and those that were left degenerated – or were allowed to degenerate – into slums. Their demise, seen at the time as both desirable and necessary, is a tragically familiar story for many of Scotland's old towns, whose disappearance in the name of 'progress' was often pursued with the kind of zeal that stifled any sort of vision. Old Bridge Street survives as a name, but the stump that is left gives no indication of what was clearly once a lively thoroughfare, albeit in a poor part of town.

The Kirkgate has survived as a street line, although the buildings in this picture have all gone, with the exception of the very fine town house in the centre. This was built in 1695 by master mason Tobias Bauchop and his initials, along with those of his wife, can be seen carved in stone between the two centre first floor windows. There is a carved sundial above them and below a group of three windows, the centre one of which was doubtless where the door would originally have been. Certainly it has been reinstated there and the building has been fully restored in a scheme part-funded by the district council and the National Trust for Scotland. The church spire in the distance is that of St Mungo's, in Bedford Place. However, the church that the Kirkgate takes its name from is the old parish church of St Mungo, which dates from 1680. Tobias Bauchop had a hand in its building too and would have seen it at close quarters from his house, diagonally across the street.

Scottish tower houses are often, and usually wrongly, called castles, but for some unknown reason Alloa's 'castle' is called a tower (so too, incidentally, are those at Clackmannan and Sauchie). Alloa Tower is a magnificent structure probably built in the late fourteenth century, but certainly sometime between 1363 when Sir Robert Erskine was granted the lands, and 1497 when it is first referred to in written records. It may have had an early function as one of a string of fortified structures along the north shore of the Forth, guarding vulnerable river crossings, but it was mainly used as a house. The Earls of Mar lived in it from the time it was built until the beginning of the nineteenth century. Over those years it was extensively modified as the focal point of beautifully landscaped pleasure grounds. The interior was remodelled and windows were slapped through the massive walls, with some fake ones also imposed on the facade to create the impression of regular fenestration. A large mansion house was built as an extension on one side in the late seventeenth century, but when this was destroyed by fire in 1800 the old tower was left isolated. As industry grew, it began to encroach on the old tower until eventually Paton's mills came to within a few yards of it. The building fell into a poor state of repair and by the 1980s decay had reached a point where its survival was in question. As is so often the case, a voluntary group, the Clackmannanshire Field Studies Society, led the fight-back. It was taken up in 1988 by the district council which along with the Earl of Mar and Kellie formed the Alloa Tower Building Preservation Trust. A restoration scheme, with funding contributions from numerous agencies, began in 1990 and the tower was officially reopened in 1997 by Her Majesty the Queen. It is now managed by the National Trust for Scotland, in partnership with Clackmannanshire Council.

ALLOA HOUSE.

After the fire in 1800, which destroyed the mansion attached to Alloa Tower, the Earl of Mar lived in a house to the west of Lime Tree Walk, but in 1838 he moved into a new mansion known as Alloa Park or Alloa House. It took four years to build, with stone quarried from within the surrounding parkland, and was about 200 yards east of Alloa Tower, facing south. The building was 120 feet across the front and 185 feet deep, and enclosed a courtyard which was entered through an arched opening. It was extensively modified in the 1850s and an adjacent stable block was also built in 1852. While this still exists, the great mansion was vacated and demolished in 1959.

Broad Street was originally known as John's Street after 'Bobbing John', the 6th Earl of Mar, whose leadership of the Jacobite Rebellion in 1715 ended in defeat and exile in France. The street was his creation as part of plans for a new town and as a grand route to and from the harbour. It is certainly broad, but that breadth, along with St John's Episcopal Church on the right and the building next to it, are about all that can now be recognised from this view taken around 1900. At that time the east side of the street was only built up at the town end, because most of its length down to the harbour was taken up with the boundary wall to the grounds surrounding Alloa House. Part way down, the so-called Earl's Gate, with its ornate cast iron gates and stone pillars, formed a grand entrance to the house and grounds. The west side of the street was more built up, with individual houses continuing down to the harbour along most of its length.

Going down towards the harbour, Bobbing John's grand street is known as Lime Tree Walk after the avenue of trees that form a walkway at its centre. The trees were planted about 1714 to make a remarkable and quite delightful feature, although one that lost its purpose when the harbour closed and people had no reason to walk that way. The avenue now has a forlorn and sorry look about it, as if waiting for some new riverside attraction to rekindle the life it once had. People walking up and down between the trees at the time this early twentieth century picture was taken could refresh themselves at a combined drinking fountain and horse trough at the town end of the avenue. Those with a serious thirst could amble down Lime Tree Walk to the Mar Inn at the harbour.

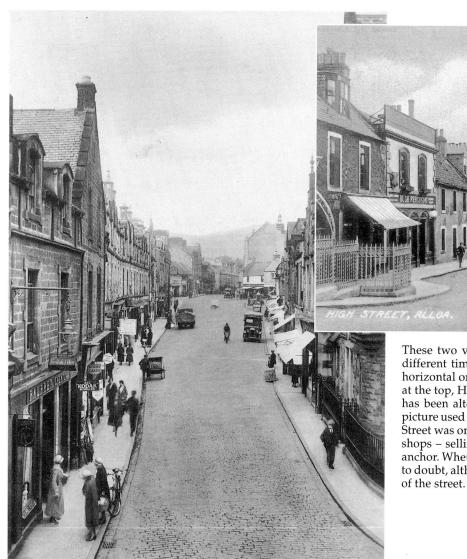

HIGH STREET, ALLOA.

These two views of High Street show it from either end, although at different times. The vertical picture dates from the mid-1930s and the horizontal one from 30 years earlier. Narrow at the foot and broadening at the top, High Street still has the feel of an old street, although the line has been altered at the top where the railing on the left of the earlier picture used to enclose the entrance to an underground gents' toilet. High Street was one of Alloa's principal retailing streets with a wide variety of shops – selling everything, as the old saying goes, from a needle to an anchor. Whether an anchor could ever have been purchased there is open to doubt, although a large one now adorns the landscaped area at the top of the street.

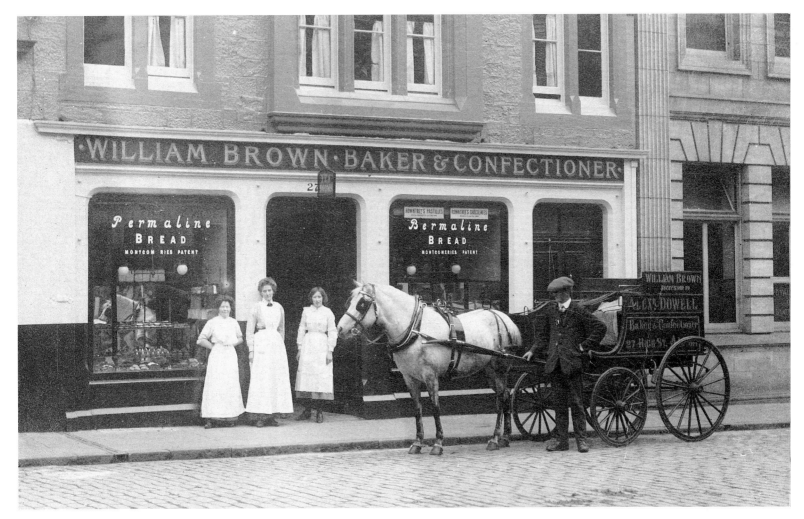

William Brown's bakery shop was situated on the left-hand side of High Street as seen in the older picture on the facing page. Brown's took over the business from Alexander Dowell whose attractively turned out vans were apparently well-known in the town. Perhaps the one in the picture, which bears the Dowell name, was one of those. The Royal Bank building alongside Brown's was built in 1909 and has been modernised since. An off-license and a building society now occupy the site where the bakery once stood.

HIGH STREET AND THE CORNER, ALLOA

The Co-op dominates this view of the top of High Street. Its building on the left was opened in 1912 to commemorate the golden jubilee of the Alloa Co-operative Society and the large SCWS sign on the gable wall to the right advertises its premises in Primrose Street. High Street and Primrose Street form a crossroads with Drysdale Street at a point where it takes a slight bend. The intersection is known as 'The Corner', but which of the many corners gave it the name? The shop, formerly a newsagents, on the corner of Primrose Street and Drysdale Street has claimed the title. On the Drysdale Street corner with High Street, tucked in behind the Co-op, was the Townhead Institute, a building dating from the time when the remarkable Catherine Forester-Paton was promoting a temperance agenda in this brewery town. She bought the popular Prince of Wales pub, demolished it and had the institute built on the site. It opened in 1914 as YWCA rooms, the same year that Miss Forester-Paton died, but continued to serve its intended purpose until 1971.

Candleriggs.

If the 'Corner' is at the top of the High Street, the 'Cross' is at the top end of Candleriggs where it forms a crossroads with Mill Street and Mar Street. This was where Alloa folk used to gather at Hogmanay to see in the new year and is marked today by pink-coloured slabs set into the road surface. The crossed slabs also mark the spot where a policeman used to stand directing traffic through this once busy part of the town. This picture looks from Mar Street into Candleriggs with Mill Street running across the foreground. The large shop on the left was a grocery which was later taken over by Sir Thomas Lipton's chain of stores and on the opposite corner was a shoe shop. Candleriggs is one of the few old Scots street-names remaining in Alloa, although not many of the buildings in this view looking towards Paton's Mills have survived with it.

Although this pre-First World War view shows Mill Street with only a parked van, it was the main thoroughfare through Alloa before the bypass road diverted most of the traffic. The picture looks east past the Cross – the building with the conical roof is where Lipton's store was. The Buttercup Dairy in the left foreground was the last but one shop in Mill Street before it ran into Bank Street – the last shop was a photographers. Two doors along from the dairy was Walter Thorburn's bookshop, although the name of Smith also appears on the sign here. Just beyond that is the distinctive mortar and pestle sign of a chemist's shop which at this time was owned by a John Cummings.

More traffic had appeared by the time this 1950s picture was taken. Just beyond where Murchie's van is parked on the left was the Gaumont Cinema which had an unusually plain tiled frontage and was erected on the former site of an earlier cinema, La Scala. Forte's Savoy cafe, where the Trust House Forte hotel chain had its humble beginnings, was adjacent to the earlier cinema. Mill Street was a busy shopping street as is clear from the number of shop awnings. Over the years there were boot and shoe shops, ironmongers, fruit and vegetable shops, confectioners, newsagents, barbers, gents outfitters, chemists and more. When people needed refreshment there were pubs, cafes and even a temperance hotel. The spire in the background is that of Chalmers Church in Bank Street.

Chalmers Church, situated just before the point where Bank Street runs into Mill Street, was built in the 1850s. Bank Street is thought to take its name from the building set back behind the railings at the left-hand edge of the picture. It dates from 1848 and was formerly the Commercial Bank. The larger building beyond it was built as the burgh chambers in the 1870s. There is now a large stone crest above the door although this appears to be absent from this early twentieth century picture. Between the burgh chambers and Chalmers Church is the Crown Hotel building which also dates from about 1870. Its name changed a few times in the past, being variously known as the Bruce Hotel and the Coach House Hotel. On the other side of the street is the only bank in the street now, the Clydesdale, which occupies a building dating from the 1850s.

This view of Bedford Place is dominated by two buildings. On the extreme left is the old Burgh School dating from 1875. It was later known as the South Primary School and is still used for educational purposes. The imposing church on the same side of the road is St Mungo's Parish Church, which was built between 1817 and 1819 as a replacement for the old St Mungo's church in Kirkgate. This had become unsafe and some stones from it were used in the construction of the new church. Across Bedford Place from St Mungo's, although not visible in this picture, is another imposing church, the West Church. Bedford Place is also graced by some very fine villas dating from the early decades of the nineteenth century. The house in the right foreground on the corner of Church Street was taken down and rebuilt in Alexandra Drive to make way for the war memorial.

Politics in Alloa used to be contested by Liberals and Unionists, but while their respective fortunes have faded, their former premises remain. Fittingly these Unionist Club rooms were in Union Street, on the corner with Coalgate. The building is characterised by its distinctive upper bow windows, but less prominently the walls also have two interesting eighteenth century date stones let into them; one shows tailoring implements.

The Liberal Club rooms in Mar Street were designed by local architect William Kerr. They were built in 1904, and were welcomed in a speech at the town hall delivered by future Liberal Prime Minister Sir Henry Campbell-Bannerman. John Thomson Paton, who donated the town hall, was a prominent Liberal Party supporter. He must have been keen on billiards because both the club rooms and the town hall had fine billiard rooms. As Liberal Party fortunes dipped, other uses were found for the rooms and they housed the district museum for a time.

Oakleigh, the large turreted house in the right foreground of this picture of Glebe Terrace, dates from 1890 and there are date stones ranging from 1888 to 1892 on other houses in the street. They would therefore have been comparatively new when this early twentieth century picture was taken. It looks toward Church Street from Ludgate; a view that has hardly changed, except that a present-day photographer would be unable to avoid the presence of motor vehicles.

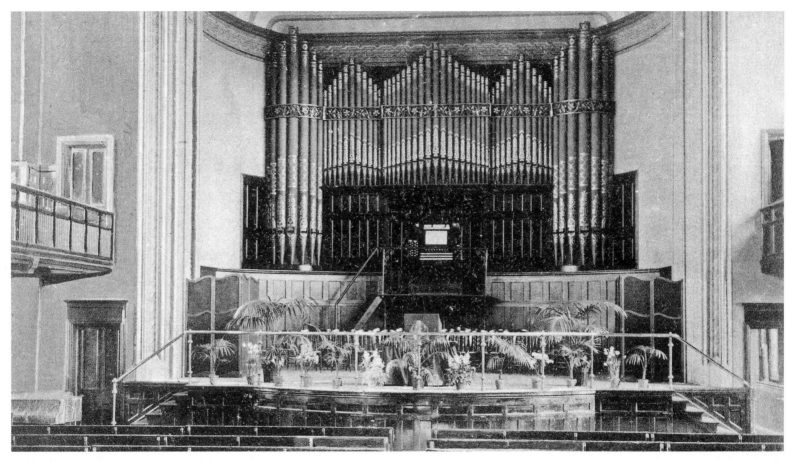

Alloa Town Hall was gifted to the burgh by John Thomson Paton of Norwood House. He engaged the London architect Alfred Waterhouse, who had also worked on the town halls of cities including Manchester and Birmingham. But if Alloa's hall was small by comparison, that did not prevent him from designing a gem of its kind. The foundation stone was laid in April 1887 and the building opened in December 1888. The large assembly hall, with its side and rear galleries, could seat 1,000 people. At the back of the stage, surmounting a pitch-pine case, was this impressive pipe organ – it was originally gas-driven, but was converted to water drive in 1902. Rooms were provided for science and art, there was a library with reading rooms and also billiard and smoking rooms. The billiard room was moved ten years later to the new baths building in Primrose Street and the vacated space taken up by the library. The library itself moved out to other premises in the 1930s. Over the years the hall has been the focus for much of Alloa's social, political and cultural life and it still fulfils that valuable purpose.

COUNTY BUILDINGS, ALLOA

214959

The Clackmannanshire County and Police Buildings were erected on the corner of Mar Street and Drysdale Street in 1863. They have been extended a couple of times since. The building edging into the picture on the extreme right has a carved plough on the pediment indicating its early life as the Plough Inn. It has now reverted to its original catering function under the name Ochil House, but during much of the nineteenth and twentieth centuries it was used by the council and the Territorial Army, who also had a large drill hall behind it. In the centre of the picture is the war memorial commemorating the men from the county who fell during the South African, or Boer, War of 1899–1902. It was erected on this site in 1904, but the protective railing surrounding it shows that by the time this picture was taken in the early 1930s it had become a hazard to the growing number of motor vehicles.

The South African War memorial was designed by Robert Lorimer and is seen here, soon after being erected, at its original site in the centre of the intersection of Mar Street, Mar Place, Marshill and Drysdale Street. When it became an impediment to traffic it was relocated to a small garden at Marshill. It was rededicated at the end of May 2002, 100 years after war ended.

Two of Alloa's well-known family names – Paton and Younger – are on the list of those who died serving in a variety of regular and colonial units, but mercifully the county appears to have been spared the worst single incident for Scottish regiments. This occurred in December 1899 during the early phase of the war when the army high command seriously underestimated the enemy and handed them the initiative – and some stunning victories. From the outset the Boers laid siege to the settlements of Kimberley and Mafeking and the British had little alternative but to attempt their relief. The troops fought their way across the Orange and Modder Rivers, but the Boers' retreat simply drew the British onto a strongly defended position at Magersfontein. The Highland Brigade, the cream of the British Army, advanced at night – standard tactics for today's sophisticated soldiers, but a seriously risky ploy then. The Highlanders were not sure exactly where the enemy was and were still moving forward in close order when the Boers opened fire at close range. Six hundred men were killed in about three minutes. The survivors took what cover they could and the battle resumed at daybreak, but it was already lost – a tragedy on a scale rarely matched by even the carnage of the First World War.

After the First World War, with so many deaths to mark, there was no single county monument and so Alloa erected a memorial of its own at the corner of Bank Street, Bedford Place and Church Street. It was unveiled by Earl Haig in 1924, and was designed by (the now knighted) Sir Robert Lorimer and topped with a sculpture by C. d'O. Pilkington-Jackson. About one in four of those commemorated by it were serving with the Argyll & Sutherland Highlanders, a reflection of the county's traditional associations with the regiment. This photograph was used as a postcard and, according to the message on the back, was taken in Alloa at Christmas time 1914. The soldiers are unknown, but it is hard to escape the melancholy thought that some of their names may be on the memorial. More were added to the lists following the Second World War.

Interior, Public Baths, Alloa.

The Co-op was the dominant commercial presence in Primrose Street selling bread and cakes from its own bakery, household furnishings and footwear. The other principal building in the street was the public baths which, like the town hall, was gifted by the beneficent John Thomson Paton. It was opened in 1898. Generations of youngsters from all over the wee county learned to swim in this splendid pond with its tiled surrounds, diving dale, hanging baskets and poolside changing cubicles. The building also contained Turkish and private baths, a gymnasium and the billiard tables which were moved across from the town hall to create more space there for the library.

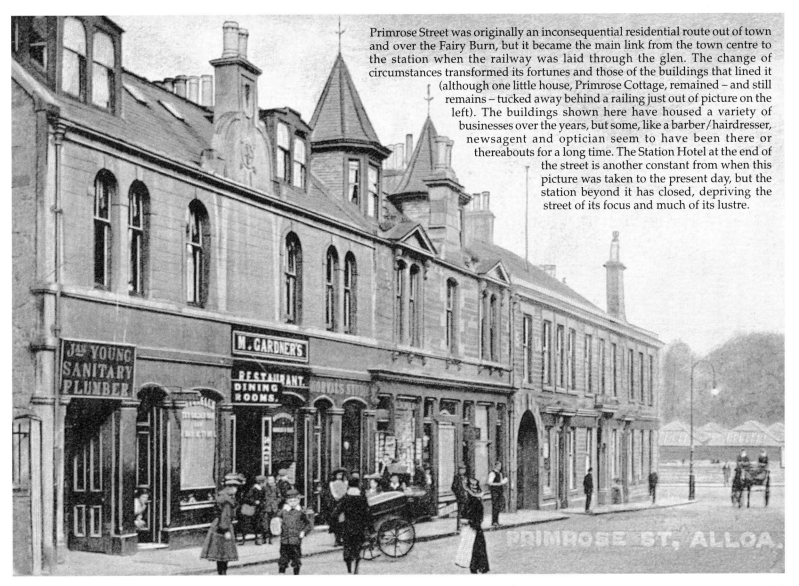

Primrose Street was originally an inconsequential residential route out of town and over the Fairy Burn, but it became the main link from the town centre to the station when the railway was laid through the glen. The change of circumstances transformed its fortunes and those of the buildings that lined it (although one little house, Primrose Cottage, remained – and still remains – tucked away behind a railing just out of picture on the left). The buildings shown here have housed a variety of businesses over the years, but some, like a barber/hairdresser, newsagent and optician seem to have been there or thereabouts for a long time. The Station Hotel at the end of the street is another constant from when this picture was taken to the present day, but the station beyond it has closed, depriving the street of its focus and much of its lustre.

Railways came to Alloa in 1850 with the opening of the Stirling & Dunfermline Railway. The town had of course been familiar with rails since the 1760s when the wagonway from the Sauchie pits was brought through the town. But while that was just used to haul coal to the harbour, the new line was different, providing people and businesses with a speedy way of getting to and from the outside world. It also started a process which, oddly for a place sandwiched between the huge natural barriers of the Forth and the Ochil Hills, made Alloa into a busy junction. Branch lines radiated to the harbour, to Cambus and Alva, to Kincardine and along the Devon Valley through Tillicoultry and Dollar to Kinross. These lines were made by small companies that had all been absorbed into the North British Railway by the mid-1870s, but it was their great rivals, the Caledonian Railway, that made the last major link into Alloa in 1885 by extending their Larbert to South Alloa line across the Forth on a new bridge. The town's station was remodelled in the late nineteenth century to cater for all these services, but then suffered from the all too familiar story of incremental closures of branch lines until the main line too was closed in 1968.

Alloa locomotive shed was to the east of the station alongside the line to Dunfermline, which runs across the foreground of this picture. The tank locomotive in front of the shed was built in Glasgow as one of a class introduced in 1904. On its side is the symbol adopted by British Railways soon after nationalisation in 1948, suggesting a probable 1950s date for the picture. The fenced embankment behind the locomotive was for the wagonway from the Sauchie and Devon Collieries. Its route down to the docks took it across a bridge over the main-line tracks and behind the loco shed, after which it dipped and curved to run between Izatt Street and the station at street level. It crossed the top of Primrose Street and turned down behind the Station Hotel where the town's coal fauld (yard) was located. Some of the trucks were unloaded there for local supplies. Part of the wagonway route from the back of the Station Hotel to the docks still exists as a cycleway and walkway.

Forth Bridge, Alloa

The Scottish Central Railway from Greenhill near Bonnybridge to Perth was a remarkably far-sighted development that formed the spine of the Scottish rail network. It was opened in 1848 and a branch from its core station at Larbert, to South Alloa, was completed in 1850, only a week after the Stirling & Dunfermline line had opened to Alloa itself. People therefore had the option of either crossing the Forth by ferry to catch a train, or going round by Stirling. In the great railway amalgamations of the 1860s, the Scottish Central was taken over by the Caledonian Railway Company which set up a separate company in 1879 to extend the South Alloa branch across the Forth on a new bridge. The result was this impressive 540 yard long structure of lattice girders set on masonry piers which was opened in 1885. The bridge also had a 60 foot opening span for shipping, but the tides, flows and cross-currents of the Forth made navigation through it an extreme test of boat handling skill. Skippers had to drive through on full power to maintain their line, and with the tide behind them this could mean shooting through a gap not much wider than the boat itself at 25–30 miles an hour. The iron girders were removed in the early 1970s after the cessation of rail traffic.

The quarter-mile river ferry crossing was affected by strong tides and currents that could sweep boats well off line before they reached the opposite jetty. Despite that it had existed for centuries before the 1860s when its operators, the Caledonian Railway Company, almost stopped running it. They used the boat to connect with their South Alloa railhead, but began to neglect it while pushing the idea of a railway bridge. The Earl of Mar and Kellie persuaded them to keep going and a new boat, the *Countess of Kellie*, was put on the crossing. When the bridge opened a local boat-builder, Alex McLeod, started to operate a new ferry, the *Lord Erskine*, replacing her in 1905 with the boat in this picture, the *Hope*, a 63 foot twin-screw steamer. She was later fitted with ramps for loading cars, but the opening of the Kincardine Bridge in 1936 spelled the end. *Hope* stopped running the following year and an attempt to keep the service going with a passenger vessel called *Sunbeam* ceased at the end of 1939.

South Alloa, on the other side of the river, wasn't just a tiny village ferry terminal. Remarkably, it was for a time Scotland's largest port for the import of pit props, or 'trees' as miners called them. Ships from the Baltic and Scandinavia unloaded at jetties and a sawmill prepared the timber for distribution to the country's pits and mines. Alloa men employed there used the ferry daily to cross to their work, while girls from Stirlingshire towns and villages who worked in Alloa went in the opposite direction. Alloa itself had existed as a port long before the wagonway from the Sauchie pits was laid to the old harbour. The Forth estuary had been one of the principal coal exporting areas of the British Isles prior to that, and the wagonway ensured that Alloa's share of that kept on growing. It increased again after the mid-1770s when the Forth & Clyde Canal gave access to the burgeoning Glasgow market. Coal exports more than doubled from Alloa after the opening of the new dock in 1885, but this dramatic increase was cut back a few years later when the development of ports like Methil and Burntisland started to make inroads into Alloa's markets. The old harbour became the province of small fishing boats which did a roaring trade in flounders. They operated in sufficient numbers for the boats to be able to sport AA – the first and last letters of Alloa – as their port of registry.

At Alloa Harbour

Alloa also developed an extensive waterfront, as this picture from 1919 shows. It was needed to meet the demands of ships and barges bringing industry's raw materials in and taking finished products out. A shipbuilding and repairing industry existed for a number of years, and excursion steamers called regularly at the port. The wharves on the river were limited in their use by tides and silting and so the wet dock at Forthbank (seen on the front cover) was developed. It was still being used by sufficient traffic in the 1930s to warrant an opening span on the Kincardine Bridge, but by the 1950s trade had dwindled to almost nothing. Despite that, the dock was upgraded. The cold war was at its height and Alloa was one of a number of small ports that were improved in case the country's major docks were put out of action by a nuclear strike. Railways were re-laid, surfaces improved and fences erected, but the bomb never came and even if it had the bridges downstream would probably have been knocked out, rendering the investment at Alloa useless! The last major cargo, a large stainless steel vessel for the Skol brewery, arrived in 1953 and the dock was later filled in. The whole waterfront descended into a sad, silted scene of dereliction, but the growth of leisure boating might yet give Alloa's river front a new lease of life.

Extensions to Alloa House pleasure grounds in the late eighteenth century required some property on the south side of the old town to be demolished. By way of compensation, John Francis Erskine, Earl of Mar, feued some land on the west side of the colliery wagonway for a new town. Its proximity to the river was clearly an incentive for shipbuilder Alexander Mustard to be the first to build a house; its foundation stone was laid in 1785. Not everyone, however, was as keen as Mustard and it was many years before his lead was followed by local architect John Smith. He built some houses in Forth Street in the nineteenth century which were followed by others spreading from the east along Forth Street and Castle Street. This view shows Forth Street looking to the east with, at the far end, what appears to be Linden House in front of the trees of Lime Tree Walk.

FORTH STREET, ALLOA

FORTH STREET, ALLOA

There are many possible reasons why the idea of a new town failed to catch on. Perhaps people saw the wagonway as a barrier and were reluctant to move across it, or the distance from the old town was a disincentive, or maybe would-be developers were deterred by the proximity of Alloa's growing industry. And it was certainly close as this view looking west along Forth Street to the glassworks shows. The houses would also have had an unobstructed view of the docks! The Customs House was halfway along Forth Street and the Ferry Inn was at the east end.

Alloa's one big industrial survivor is the glassworks. It was, like so many of the town's eighteenth century developments, an idea hatched by the 6th Earl of Mar. While in exile, he travelled widely in Europe and noted that the raw materials needed for a bottle-work were available in the vicinity of Alloa: sand, coal, kelp from the lower Forth estuary and salt from Kennetpans. But while the idea may have been his, it was the dynamic and forceful Lady Frances Erskine who set up the works in 1750. She brought in experienced workers from Europe to make bottles which were supplied to wine importers, principally at Leith, who were required by law to bring wine into the country in casks before decanting it into bottles for sale. After keeping the enterprise going for a few difficult years, Lady Frances transferred control in 1767 to a partnership of local merchants and they, and their successors, have kept it going ever since. Extensive mechanisation after the Second World War achieved a five-fold increase in production, including the supply of 80 per cent of the country's milk bottles. The works, now operated by United Glass, has been in operation on its original site longer than any other glassworks in Europe. A brick cone from the early nineteenth century has also been preserved on the site.

The Mills Brewery off Old Bridge Street was set up by a John McDermid about 1804. It was leased by James Maclay in 1830 and in 1871, after he had moved into his new Thistle Brewery, the lease was taken over by Robert Henderson. He died in 1897, but his sons George and Thomas carried on running the business, buying the brewery outright and trading under the name of R. Henderson & Co. Ltd. from 1909. They produced a bulk beer in casks, and ale and stout in bottles, but latterly the last surviving son, George, was keeping the brewery going on his own and production was small. Operations ceased in 1941 when George Henderson died, and although the somewhat run-down premises were taken over by James Calder & Co. Ltd. they were eventually demolished. The identity of the man standing in front of the brewery in this picture is not known.

The neat little terrace of houses that makes up one side of Dirleton Gardens has hardly changed since these pictures were taken in or before 1907, when one view was used as a postcard. The trees with their encircling railings have gone and some modern improvements have been made, but the major change to the street took place in 1921 when the first council houses in Alloa were built opposite the little terrace. The boggy field where the new housing was built is not visible in these pictures, but in the background on the extreme left of the main picture is a large private mansion (now demolished) known as Norwood House. It was built in 1874 and belonged to John Thomson Paton.

The West End Park was feued from the Earl of Mar and Kellie and opened by Chief Magistrate, William Bailey, on 1 May 1878. Football goalposts are the most conspicuous evidence of modern sporting endeavour at the park, but the 'beautiful game' was not always such a dominant sporting force, as these young cricketers show. Cricket was popular in Scotland before football took over and it has continued to enjoy a following in the area. The Clackmannanshire County Cricket Club, now based at the Arns, was formed about 1860, and succeeded in winning the Scottish Counties Championship in 1924. The railway cutting, now used by the bypass road connecting Marshill to Glasshouse Loan, is just beyond the trees, and the chimneys of the town hall can be seen on the left, with Paton's chimney and the spire of St Mungo's to the right.

This picture of Mar Place was sent as a postcard to London in 1908. Part of the message on the back suggests that the recipient 'will know what street that is' which is just as well because there is no title on the card. Now there are no buildings left to identify the picture; Parkway Court and Ludgate House occupy the ground vacated by them, and the new road known as Parkway joins Mar Place where the entrances on the right of the picture were. The one on the extreme right led down to the goods yard beside Alloa station. Alongside that, where the little group of people have gathered below the gas lamp, was the entry to David Kellock's blacksmith's yard.

The Mar Place houses on the facing page backed onto the grounds of Greenfield House which extended along Mar Place and Tullibody Road to a dog-legged extension of Hill Street, known as Viewfield Place. This name had been dropped in favour of the whole street being called Hill Street by the time this view looking toward Tullibody Road was taken early in the twentieth century. The buildings on the right have now all been replaced, but those on the left remain and the old Co-operative store on the edge of the picture is still a small grocery. The trees on the left stood in part of the grounds of Greenfield House which adjoined a large ropeworks running at the back of the main line of Hill Street.

The builders of these cottages in Tullibody Road would have been surprised that the trend they began at the start of the twentieth century would see the road built up almost as far as Tullibody itself by the end of the century. Otherwise there has been little change to this part of the road, although the trees on the south side are now incorporated into the footpath and do not, as here, stick out into the road caged by steel surrounds. The street coming in on the left is Paton Street.

Paton Street, seen here looking towards Tullibody Road, has also changed little since this view was taken sometime before 1907 when it was used as a postcard. The picture might indeed have been taken to show the newly completed street, because only a few houses at the top end had been built before 1900 and the rest must therefore have been erected in the few intervening years. Many more houses now clothe the rising ground beyond Tullibody Road.

PATON'S SPORTS PAVILION AND PLEASURE GROUNDS, ALLOA.

A 377

Patons & Baldwins established a staff sports complex beside the Tullibody Road beyond Victoria Street, and erected a fine pavilion there in 1926 to the designs of William Kerr. The opening was marked with bowling and tennis matches, and a game of cricket between Paton's and Bonnybridge Cricket Club. With the demise of the company some of the grounds have been built on, but the bowling green and the pavilion survive.

Inglewood is a large mansion set back from Tullibody Road. When it was built in 1900 it was in open countryside surrounded by woods, but Alloa's inexorable growth eventually spread out to surround the house. It was gifted to the Church of Scotland as an eventide home, a home for elderly people, by Alexander Forester-Paton and is now used as a business centre.

THE GEAN HOUSE, ALLOA, HALL LOUNGE AND INGLE NEUK   3

Further out towards Tullibody, on the other side of the road from Inglewood, was an area of woodland which gave its name to another great mansion, The Gean. This was built in 1912 by Alexander Forester-Paton's parents as a wedding gift to him. They commissioned local architect, William Kerr, who designed many stylish buildings in and around Alloa. The house is now used as a conference centre.

Erskine Street originally ran from the railway station up to Ashley Terrace, but only a short section of it now survives along with a cut-off end giving access to the footbridge over the railway cutting. Behind the fence on the left of this view from the station end is the yard of a monumental sculptor, whose close proximity to Sunnyside Cemetery no doubt helped to keep him in business. The buildings in the distance are on the corners where Erskine Street intersects with Hill Street and beyond that with Queen Street. Those in the right foreground are on the corner of Greenfield Street.

Greenfield Street, like Erskine Street, was lined on both sides with tenements rising out of narrow pavements. On the right-hand side at the far end was a builder's yard which belonged at one time to G. & R. Cousin who built the town hall. They were presumably also responsible for erecting the tenements opposite the yard known as Cousin's Buildings. Also on the right-hand side was a foundry, an abattoir, Paton's wool store and a block known as the Victoria and Albert Buildings. Beyond the building on the left of the picture was a stables, a joiner's shop, a coal yard and a laundry. These stark tenements and unattractive businesses are a pointer to the poor economic circumstances of this part of town. A little girl sitting against a lamp-post perhaps makes the point better than words can that for some people the old days were often not good!

CO-OPERATIVE SPORTS GROUNDS, ALLOA. 98/12

The little girl in the previous picture would no doubt have attended Sunnyside School. It was erected in Erskine Street in 1892 and has seen generations of Alloa children pass through its segregated boys' and girls' entrance doors. Once inside they had to face such characters as John Ferguson, the bearded, cane wielding headmaster nicknamed the Lion Tamer. A new building which has been erected to connect with the girls' door blocks this view of the school from the Co-op bowling green. The green was set out on a field where the Co-operative Society used to graze cattle and sheep on their way to the slaughter house. The clubhouse was erected in 1925 to the designs of the architect George Kerr.

In Ashley Terrace, behind both school and clubhouse, was the Clackmannan County Hospital, which was opened in March 1899 as a gift to the county from Miss Catherine Forester-Paton, whose interest in nursing had given her a sound insight into the need for proper medical care. It was erected adjacent to an old hospital which had been in existence since 1868. The new building was designed by Robert Bryden, a Glasgow architect who worked on a number of hospitals, and had a male and a female ward, private rooms, a small operating theatre and a central administration block. The picture shows the male ward in the 1950s. The hospital still functions within the NHS as a general hospital although local people have always referred to it as the 'accidents' hospital.

ALLOA FOOTBALL CLUB

Alloa Athletic Football Club was formed in 1878 and after playing at Gaberston and Bellvue Parks moved to their present ground, Recreation Park, in 1895. The club was admitted to the Scottish League's newly formed Second Division in 1921 and by winning it gained promotion in the first season. Unable to sustain this elevated status they were back in the Second Division by season 1938/39 when they again won promotion, as runners-up to Cowdenbeath, but were denied the chance to consolidate their place at the top when the following season was cancelled due to the Second World War. After the war, when the league started up again, the 'Wasps' – so called because of their yellow and black hooped shirts – were placed in what was called Division B – effectively a second division. They have remained out of the top flight ever since, but with the team winning promotion to Division One for season 2002/03 the prospects are looking up, at least for another year! This team came fourth in the old Second Division in season 1935/36. They are: *Back row*: D. Cadden (trainer), J. Richardson, J. Reid (match secretary), J. Kerr (captain), R. Muir, W. Crawford (director), J. Beath, J. McMullen, J. Irvine, J. Polland, J. Mathieson (financial secretary). *Front row*: R. Shankley, T. Williamson, J. Foley, R. Duffey, J. Halliday.